SANGMA FRANCIS

RÔMOLO D'HIPÓLITO

AMAZON RIVER

FLYING EYE BOOKS
LONDON | LOS ANGELES

CONTENTS

INTRODUCTION

High up in the Andes mountains of South America, a drop of water wells up from the ground. It collects and glistens downwards, cutting along the side of mountains. It joins larger streams, weaves and washes through overgrown forests. Finally, after traveling for thousands of miles, it ends at the sea.

This is a story that has a tiny beginning and a mighty end! The Amazon River is a place where pink dolphins swim, manatees have been mistaken for mermaids, where fish eat flesh, and meadows float. It is the story of a body of water that connects each tiny thing in the great rainforest around it, the most biodiverse place on Earth. Like a drop of water, together we will dip, flow, crash, and slide into pages of animals, insects, trees, and people that all use the river in different ways. We will discover the importance of the river and all that surrounds it.

Welcome to Nature's palace.

FROM SOURCE TO SEA

HOW LARGE IS LARGE?

The Amazon is the world's largest river. It stretches across seven countries and is 4,000 miles long. Around it grows the world's largest rainforest, which greedily devours the river's water. When we say the Amazon is the world's largest river, it means it pumps out the most water.

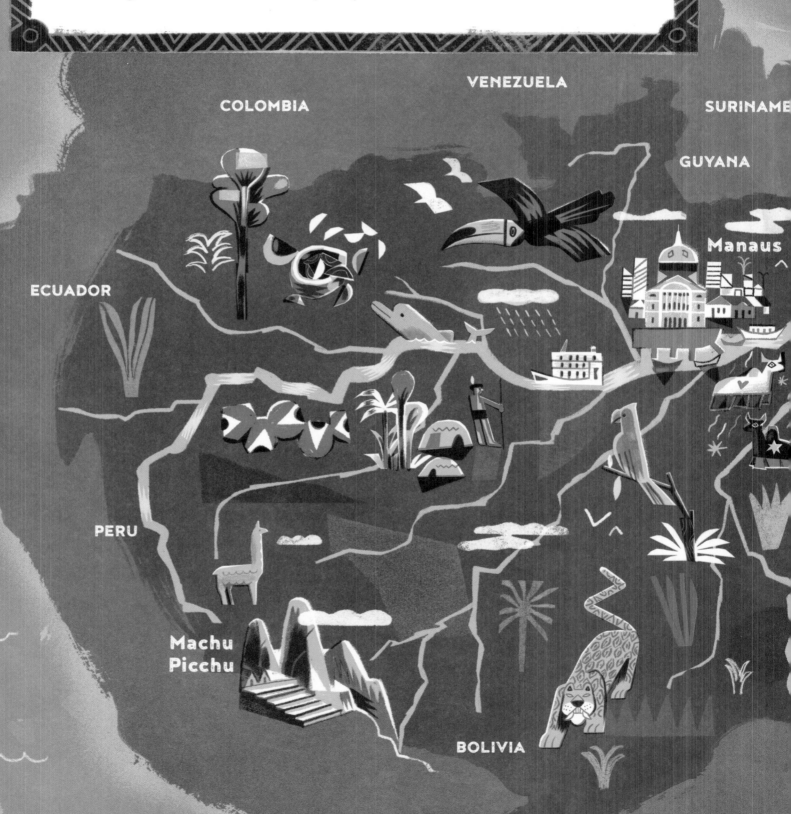

COLOMBIA

VENEZUELA

SURINAME

GUYANA

Manaus

ECUADOR

PERU

Machu Picchu

BOLIVIA

THE AMAZON BASIN

The land around the river network is called a **basin**. The Amazon basin is the world's largest river basin at over 2.4 million square miles. Across such an enormous amount of space, the water can be very different from one place to another. Different types of water will be more attractive to different flowers and birds, trees and insects, fish and mammals.

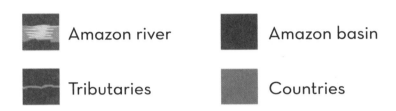

Amazon river

Amazon basin

Tributaries

Countries

TRIBUTARIES

Every river is made from a network of smaller rivers called **tributaries**. This tangled collection of waterways makes a network. The Amazon has over 1,100 tributaries, which flow to its main trunk. Tributaries can be tiny streams, barely visible from afar, or they can be huge in their own right.

WHERE DOES IT ALL START?

Once upon a time, expeditions tried to follow the river back to its source by walking along the riverbank. Now, using satellites, we can map river systems. Yet we still don't know where it all starts!

Not only is the Amazon huge, there are different ideas about what we can call a source. A river can be measured from the first trickle of water to join it, or the first tributary with a constant flow all year round. Since some dry up in summer, the source is still a source of disagreement.

WATER, WATER, WATER

Rivers like the Amazon are made of fresh water. Fresh water is enormously important to all life. Plants would wither and die without it and humans would not exist. It is one of the most extraordinary things on Earth. It can freeze into ice, like arctic sheets and glaciers of the world. It can heat and rise as a gas to collect into clouds of moisture. It can be stored as lakes beneath rock or soil. Almost every great city in history has been built on a bank of fresh water. But of all the water in the world, only 3% of it is fresh water, the other 97% is salt water from the sea.

WATER TYPES

The water of the Amazon can be split into three types: clearwater, whitewater and blackwater. The difference is in the chemicals and particles they carry.

CLEARWATER

Crystal-clear clearwater runs over ancient rock in the Guiana Shield area of South America. The water sometimes flows at furious speeds and tumbles as a waterfall or swirls as rapids.

BLACKWATER

This type of water churns very slowly across forested land, sometimes so slowly you can't tell it's moving. Leaves fall into the water and rot away at the bottom, turning the water a dark, chocolatey color. Blackwater doesn't carry as many nutrients as other types and is very acidic.

WHITEWATER

Whitewater is a milky, muddy color that looks like flowing caramel. The color comes from floating sediment, broken-down pieces of rock, and tiny grains of sand, silt, and minerals that come from the erosion of the Andes Mountains.

THE WATER CYCLE

Across the Earth, water is continuously moving. Not just in the rivers and seas, but through the air too. This movement of water is called the **water cycle**, it is a natural recycling process and it has been happening for millions of years. The water that you drink may have once been slurped up by a dinosaur! The water cycle is even happening right now, all around you.

2. Into the Clouds!

When the water vapor cools down in the colder air, it transforms back into minuscule drops of liquid which makes clouds. This is called **condensation***.*

1. Evaporation

The sun heats up water in rivers, lakes, seas, and on land. This turns it into **water vapor***, changing from a liquid into a gas. The vapor rises into the air, like steam from a kettle.*

3. Down to the Ground

*When the clouds get heavy and full of vapor, they fall back to the ground. This could look like rain, sleet, snow, or hail. Its scientific name is **precipitation**.*

4. Back to Earth

The falling water runs into the ground or back out to sea. It is gulped up by plants, humans, and animals. Back on land the cycle starts over again.

BREATHING TREES

Trees and plants get plenty of water from growing along the river. With so much liquid everywhere, the plants have enough to survive. They add to the water cycle in their own way by breathing out water vapor (**transpiration**). The Amazon basin adds 6.5 trillion gallons of water to the atmosphere each day!

WATERFALLS

Waterfalls are channels of water that fall off a steep ledge and plunge into a pool below. They often form when water flows from soft rock to hard rock. The soft rock erodes, leaving a ledge that the stream tumbles over. Waterfalls can also form at cracks in the Earth's surface, from earthquakes, landslides, glaciers, and volcanoes.

WHIRLPOOLS

A whirlpool is a pool of water that rotates quickly into itself. This usually happens when two different currents meet or when water crashes against a barrier. In a river, this could be a jutting bit of land or water flowing in a different direction. A whirlpool that can suck things underwater is called a vortex.

TWIST, TUMBLE, AND FALL

Where the ground is higher, the rivers usually flow much faster. Water flow can change depending on weather, like rain, and temperature which affects melting glaciers. These swirling and whirling rivers are not easy to navigate. They can wreck a boat in a matter of minutes, especially where the water is shallow and rocks jut sharply from the surface.

RAPIDS

Rapids are fast-flowing waters in a stream, which can be extremely rough and wild. Rapids usually happen in shallow waters where there are more rocks for the waters to slap against and swirl around. The movement from rapids traps a lot of oxygen from the air, which is good for fish since they breathe through their gills.

GORGES

A gorge is a deep, thin valley that cuts into earth and rock. They are usually made by rivers that erode the rock over thousands of years. Gorges can also be formed by large movements in the surface of the Earth, such as an earthquake.

THREE RIVERS

The Amazon River is not the only river to feed the land around it. There are three different types of river in the Amazon basin. The other two are not what you might expect! One is deep underground below the river you can see. The other flows above it, through the sky, and moves in the other direction.

AERIAL RIVER

The plants of the Amazon rainforest suck moisture up from the soil and when the sun comes up, they breathe it out into the air. Great clouds of water vapor rise like mist from millions of trees and plants. It forms an aerial (airborne) river that flows towards the mountains. The water vapor falls back down as rain in the Amazon and beyond.

SURFACE RIVER

This is the river you can see. Surface water builds up from precipitation (rain) and melting ice and snow from nearby mountains. For the Amazon river, this comes from the Andes. It is the longest mountain range in the world, stretching 4,350 miles to form South America's spine. The mountains are also home to 90% of the world's tropical glaciers (slow-moving rivers of ice).

HAMZA RIVER

Beneath the surface of the Amazon river, over two miles down, another river flows. It is called the Hamza river and has only recently been discovered. It is 3,700 miles long, nearly as long as the surface river, but much, much wider. It is between 120 and 250 miles wide! Scientists discovered the river through a series of large wells in the forest.

FLOODED FORESTS

In the wet season, heavy tropical rain fills up the river. The rainy season begins at different times across South America. The rising water is like a pulse, spreading and receding throughout the year. At its height, the flood can stretch up to 30 miles wide, while in the dry season, animals must creep out of the forest to drink from the depleted river.

TREES UNDERWATER

Flooded forests of black water are called the Igapó. For six to eight months of the year, trees are completely swallowed up beneath the water, which can rise up to 20 feet deep. Traveling through, you might only see the top of trees, like small green clouds blooming on the surface. The extreme conditions mean trees must adapt. Some have buttress roots (large, thick roots on the surface) to keep steady, while others have roots that grow into the air. Their seeds can also survive a long time in the water, unlike other plant seeds, which would rot.

SEED CARRIERS

Trees in flooded forests bloom in the flood season. Their seeds are then eaten by animals who spread them **downstream**. Pygmy marmosets are one such animal. These tiny monkeys like to drink sap from trees and gobble down their nuts and fruit.

FLOWER FIELDS

During the wet months, whitewater rivers flood to create areas called várzeas. The várzeas are full of nutrients. When the land is underwater, different types of flora appear on the surface of the water to form floating meadows. These are thick plant mats with their roots partly anchored in the soil, that sit and drift with the water. Once they begin to grow, these plants can cover double the area in just two weeks.

Water lettuce

Water hyacinths
(Eichornia crassipes)

Paspalum repens,
Echinochloa polystachya

QUEEN OF LILIES

The Victoria regia lily grows in the várzea forest. Its large, thick leaves can grow over six feet wide! The top surface of the lily has a waxy layer that repels water, while its underbelly has sharp spines to protect it from nibbling fish. The leaves have ribs with pockets of air trapped within that make them float. It only blooms at night.

THE RIVER MOUTH

Muddy water flushes out of the river mouth 90 miles off the coast of Brazil before blending fully with the sea. If a sailor cupped their hands to taste the water in this area, they'd find it isn't salty. The Amazon river pumps out 58 million gallons of water every second—a fifth of the world's fresh water. Its **estuary** is home to an enormous island, small sandy islets, and mangrove forests. It is the world's largest river mouth.

REEF

RIVER MOUTH

MARAJO ISLAND

MARAJO ISLAND

Marajo Island is one of the world's largest river islands. It was created over thousands of years from sediment carried down from the Andes. It is bigger than Switzerland and covered in dense forest and tropical savannah.

Each year, over half of the island is flooded, yet the amount of wildlife that lives here is astounding. There are 361 species of bird and 99 species of mammal, including jaguars and water buffalo.

TIDAL BORE

The Amazon is home to the world's most famous **tidal bore**. It's called the pororoca and it sweeps back up the river just before the spring tides each year. A tidal bore creates a wave that speeds back **upstream**, working against the current. The pororoca travels up to 15 miles per hour, and rises up to 13 feet high! Surfers gather each year to catch a ride, and if they're lucky they'll go all 620 miles upstream with the pororoca.

CORAL REEF

A huge colorful coral reef expands 3,600 square miles across the river's mouth. It is over 200 feet deep and is home to a curious array of colorful fish, tiny marine worms, brittle stars, and huge sea sponges. Coral usually only grows in seawater so it was a surprise for scientists to discover a reef growing here, where the water isn't as salty as normal due to the fresh water from the river.

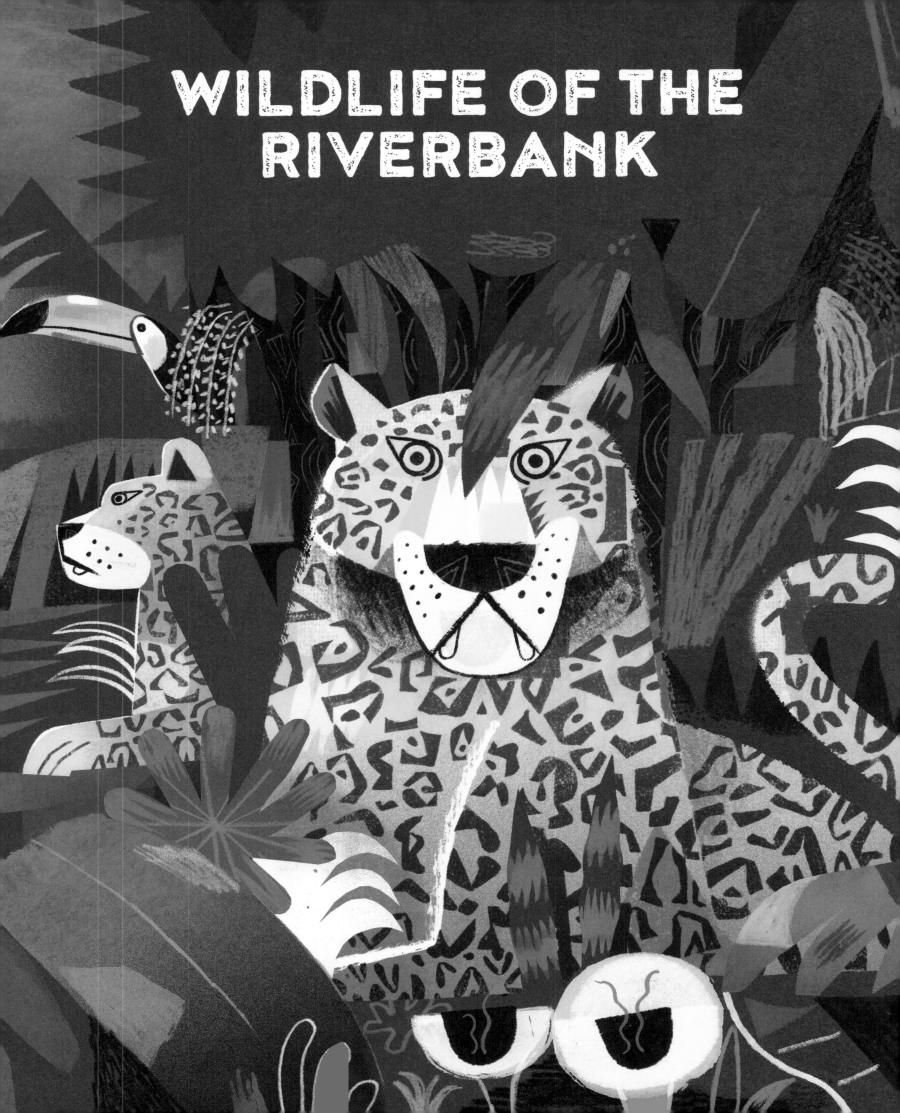

WILDLIFE OF THE RIVERBANK

RIVERSIDE ECOSYSTEM

An **ecosystem** is like a tiny environment where living and non-living things work together. Non-living things might be the soil, water, or temperature. Living things will be the plants, insects, or animals. Each of these rely on each other. Animals and plants in the Amazon have evolved for thousands of years to work very well in their ecosystem. If one thing, like a plant, becomes **extinct** then the animal that eats it won't survive. This makes an ecosystem a very fragile system.

FOOD WEBS

The Amazon is the most **biodiverse** place on Earth. The animals that live in habitats in and along the river are all part of a food chain that in turn connects to make a food web. Food webs show us how each living thing relies on others to live. Like all food webs across the world, those of the Amazon have four different parts.

1. The Growers

Primary producers are the living things that make food for the rest. In the Amazon these could be trees, grasses, reeds, or flowers like bromeliads.

2. The Vegetarians

Primary consumers are the animals that eat the plants. In the Amazon they could be macaws, toucans, monkeys, fish, agouti, sloths, or insects.

3. The Big Eaters

Secondary consumers (or predators) are animals that eat plant-eating ones. These could be a heron, dolphin, jaguar, or boa constrictor.

4. Great Rotters

Decomposers are the bacteria, insects, and fungi that break down dead things and dung. They recycle it for the plants to re-use.

AMPHIBIANS

The word amphibian means "two lives," and applies to creatures that begin their life in water then live out of it as adults. Once grown, they cannot go for long without water—luckily the Amazon forest has plenty of it. There are 427 species of amphibians in the Amazon.

POISON DART FROG

These little creatures come in many vibrant colors, and are the most toxic animals on Earth. The poison is strong enough to kill up to ten adults. They get their name from having their poison rubbed onto the tips of hunting darts and arrows.

GLASS FROG

This frog's underbelly is completely clear, making its heart and bones visible. Its transparent skin lets the color of different surfaces, like large leaves, show through, **camouflaging** it perfectly.

SALAMANDER

They use their webbed feet to easily climb trees. Salamanders breathe air but don't have lungs. Instead they absorb oxygen through their wet skin.

PARADOXICAL FROG

This frog gets its name from the strange nature of its growth. It starts as a large tadpole but over the course of its life it becomes smaller in size.

REPTILES

Animals such as snakes, lizards, crocodiles, and turtles are all reptiles. They are coldblooded so need the sun to stay warm. They have scales, which act as armor, and most lay eggs. Reptiles are some of the oldest creatures in the world—dinosaurs were a type of reptile! There are 378 species of reptiles in the Amazon.

LIZARDS

Amazonian lizards range in size from tiny geckos to the crocodile-like caiman lizard. To swim, lizards move their tails and bodies from side to side, with their limbs tucked in tightly.

Caiman lizard

The green iguana likes to bask up in the canopy or down by the water. They are quick climbers and confident swimmers.

SNAKES

These slithering creatures wrap themselves high in the trees, creep their way through the undergrowth or swim in the waters to hunt. Snakes are carnivorous so use different methods to kill their prey. Snakes will eat fish, birds, other snakes, lizards, and small rodents.

*The **aquatic** coral snake feeds on fish. Its venom is so deadly it can kill instantly!*

TURTLES

The river is home to 45 different species of freshwater turtle. They are omnivorous, eating plants and smaller animals such as shrimp.

The Arrau is one of the largest turtles. It is a type of side-necked turtle. It doesn't pull its head back into its shell but turns it and tucks it.

Yellow spotted river turtle

CAIMANS

There are six different species of caiman in the Amazon. The caiman is a part of the crocodile family that lives in swamps and rivers. Their eyes sit watchfully above the water, their bodies lying low and camouflaged beneath. They don't use their feet to swim, instead they use their powerful tails to swish forwards.

Cuvier's dwarf caiman (the smallest caiman)

Yacare Caiman

The most common type is the spectacled caiman. It has a bony ridge along its eyes that look like a pair of glasses. All the better to see you with!

FISH

The Amazon river is home to an incredible number of fish that come in all different shapes and sizes. In total there are 3,000 species of fish, and 2,000 of these are **endemic** to the Amazon waters. When describing animals, "endemic" means you can only find them in one place.

ELECTRIC EEL

Lurking in murky streams and on muddy river bottoms is the electric eel. These slithering fish are not eels at all but actually a type of catfish or knife fish. Their long tubular bodies, which can grow over six feet long, hold electric organs that take up four-fifths of their body space. At low voltage, the electricity is used to find their way in dark water. At high voltage, they can stun prey. They feed on small fish, frogs, crabs, and even birds. Electric eels breathe air, every now and then swimming up to the surface to gulp in oxygen.

PEACOCK EYE STINGRAY

These strange, flat fish move about along river beds and bury themselves into the sand. Their eyes sit on the top of the head so that when they hide they can see what's happening in the water above. Their mouths are underneath, all the better for slurping up food on the river floor. Their tails are equipped with a razor sharp, venomous barb for protection. Their bodies contain no bones, just bendy **cartilage**. They may not look like it, but these are close relatives of the shark!

THE PIRANHA

Piranhas are carnivorous fish that live throughout South America. The waterways of the Amazon river have over 20 varieties, including the famous red-bellied piranha whose teeth are razor sharp and which have incredibly strong jaws. Piranha hunt in packs of 50 to 100 and take it in turns to feed on their prey by nibbling at flesh with their scissor-like bite. Although they are attracted to the smell of blood, and can sometimes be caught in a dangerous feeding-frenzy, they don't often hunt to kill. They are most dangerous when food around them is scarce, particularly when they have been caught in pools of receding waters in the time of drought.

Red-bellied piranha

Tometes camunani

FRUITY FISH

Not all piranhas are threatening. Some simply like to nibble the scales of similar-sized fish, and others are purely vegetarian. The vegetarian piranha is called the *Tometes camunani,* and it likes to eat fruit. Fruit grows at the same time as the yearly floods and plenty falls into the water for the fish to gobble up. The seeds digest slowly and get carried a long way before the piranha shoots it out. The vegetarian piranha is one of at least 150 species of fruit-eating fish that live in the wetlands of South America and help distribute tree seeds.

AQUATIC MAMMALS

Mammals have hair and a spine, are warm-blooded, and give birth to their young. You are a mammal. So are many other animals, like dogs, cats, leopards, and rodents. The Amazon river is home to aquatic mammals, some of which are not found anywhere else in the world.

GIANT OTTER

When standing, the giant otter can reach up to 6ft tall. It lives in small rivers called creeks. Otters have webbed feet to push them through the water, their ears can close when going under, and their fur is water-repellent. Wild otters are often hunted. They are an endangered species and at risk of extinction.

PINK RIVER DOLPHIN

These dolphins really are bright pink! They have long muzzles, a melon-shaped head, and chubby cheeks. They are the only dolphin to have two different types of teeth. When the rivers flood they can sometimes be seen weaving through the trunks of the flooded forests.

CAPYBARA

The capybara is the world's largest rodent and can grow over four feet long. It is semi-aquatic and lives in the forested banks of the river, swamps, lakes, and flooded savannahs. Sometimes known as water hogs, these sweet giants swim and dive and can stay underwater for over five minutes. Their name comes from the Tupi language and means "one who eats slender leaves."

AMAZONIAN MANATEE

The Amazonian manatee has a large, rounded body, egg-shaped head and bristly, hippopotamus-like muzzle. Despite their incredible size and weight, these are gentle creatures that swim through warm, slow-moving rivers. The Amazonian species is the only manatee that can't live in salty waters. They are herbivores, only eating aquatic plants, and they spend their time eating, sleeping, and traveling. They can only spend 3 to 5 minutes underwater before coming up to breathe air. The manatee has long been hunted for its flesh and fat and has sadly become a rare sight in the rivers.

LIVING IN THE FAST LANE

Rivers in the higher mountains are fast and extremely cold. The **flora** (plants) and **fauna** (animals) have cleverly adapted to this tricky part of the river system. While few creatures can live in these waters, those that can survive here will reap the rewards of the river's nutrients.

CADDISFLY

An insect that lives out of water but lays its eggs in water for protection. The larvae of the caddisfly have hook-like structures that can cling to rocks.

SUCKERMOUTH FISH

Found in the fast-flowing streams of the Andes, this type of catfish uses its mouth to grip on to rocks. It has even been seen climbing up waterfalls.

WHITE-CAPPED DIPPER

A small black and white bird that lives near rapids and fast-flowing water. They eat insect larvae and other small creatures from the bottom of rocky streams. Their strong legs and sharp claws help them fish.

DORADO CATFISH

The dorado catfish is a phenomenal swimmer that makes a tremendous migration all the way down the Amazon river. The young fish spawn in the foothills of the Andes but find their mate at the river's mouth. When the time is right, they struggle back to the mountains against the raging currents. The journey can take them two years.

GIANTS OF THE WATER

In the river and along its banks, predators stalk, swim, and feed. The Amazon River is home to some magnificent hunters, some of which are extraordinarily large! And what better place to feast than in water that is full of things to eat?

GREEN ANACONDA

The green anaconda is the largest and heaviest snake in the world, weighing up to 550 lb. It slithers through the water, using its strength and weight to bring down its victims. The anaconda is part of the constrictor family, which means it wraps itself tightly around its victims, crushing their bones and squeezing the air out of them before swallowing them whole.

38

JAGUAR

The jaguar is one cat that does not mind the water! It lives and hunts near riverbanks. It is the largest cat in South America, with the most powerful bite. Its teeth can crack a turtle's shell, while its tongue is covered in sharp, pointed bumps to lick meat off bones.

BLACK CAIMAN

Caimans are crocodilians—dry, scaly animals that lay soft eggs on land. They are found only in Central and South America. The black caiman is the largest species, and can reach over 15 feet from tail to snout. Its eyes and nose sit on top of its head, which allows it to see and breathe in water while staying hidden.

LEGEND OF THE PIRARUCU

In the Uaias tribe of the Amazon, there is a story of a brave but arrogant warrior who enraged the gods with his pride. He was the son of the chief, yet he was cruel to the monkeys, spiders, birds, and people. The gods had grown tired of the young man's ways. While the man was out fishing, the god of thunder cracked open the skies. The goddess of rain threw down her cloak and filled the river with waves. But the man did not care and laughed at their warnings. His arrogance was paid with a greater fury: he was struck by lightning, which cast him deep into the river. There he was turned into a large, dark fish that would stalk the waters forever more. It was called the pirarucu.

PREHISTORIC PIRARUCU

Growing up to 10 feet long, the pirarucu is one of the largest freshwater fish in the world. This species is also one of the most ancient, having been around and hardly changed since the time of the Jurassic era, around 200 million years ago. It is able to lunge out of the water and knock fishermen out of their boats with its weight. Its scales are so thick and flexible that they function like armor and allow them to swim in piranha-infested lakes.

It eats plants, crustaceans, large fish, and even birds, which it crushes with its bony tongue and studded teeth. But the most spectacular feature is that unlike most fish, it breathes air. It lives close to the water's surface and reaches up for breath with a small coughing noise.

PEOPLE OF THE RAINFOREST

ANCIENT CIVILIZATIONS

The Amazon has been home to human life for 12,000 years, since the time of the last ice age. American civilizations that existed before European colonizers are called pre-Columbian. **Archaeologists** think that at one time, there might have been as many as 5 million people living throughout the Amazon rainforest. To trace where humans were and how they lived, we need clues that are left from the past. These could be bones, buildings, tools, or ornaments. In the jungle there is another clue... the trees.

REGO GRANDE

In the heart of the Brazilian jungle, a circle of huge stones has been discovered. Some people call it the Amazonian Stonehenge! It is believed to be 1,000 years old. It's not clear what it was built for, but as archaeologists have found a burial urn in the ground nearby, it may have been a cemetery.

GEOGLYPHS

As more of the rainforest is being cut back, thousands of historic geoglyphs are being discovered. A geoglyph is a large design made by people, sometimes out of stones or mounds of soil.

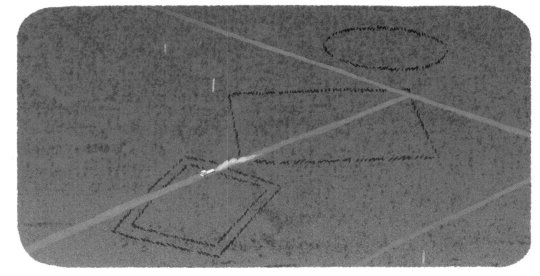

Acai berries

Peach palm fruit

THE FOREST GARDEN

Archaeologists studying the rainforest noticed that there were more trees with edible fruits than they had expected. This means people had been eating fruit and leaving the seeds behind to grow. There were trees such as peach palms, whose fronds are good for weaving rope, as well as tasty acai, brazil nuts, and cocoa.

Cocoa pods

Brazil nuts

INCA EMPIRE

The Inca reigned over a mighty empire across South America for nearly 100 years, until 1532 when Spanish invaders arrived. The Inca were famous for their great skill in building **aqueducts** and cities. They built their cities up high, where mountains were steep, forests were thick, and plains stretched far in between. Their center was in Cuzco in the Andean mountains, where they built the sacred Temple of the Sun. To the south of Cuzco lay their sacred valley, where they used ancient man-made pools to make salt for cooking. The chief Inca was called Son of the Sun.

Today, archaeologists are still uncovering hidden Inca cities in mountains and forests. They are also discovering the remains of old water roads called aqueducts. Inca workers cut through mountains, and dug channels into cliffs to bring the rivers into the cities. These aqueducts fed into baths, fountains, and fields to allow for farming and life where water was scarce.

MACHU PICCHU

Machu Picchu is an Inca city that was built above the Urubamba river and its treacherous whirlpools. The Inca were skilled stonemasons and the city is a spectacular construction of master stonework. They carved huge rocks to fit perfectly together. With the use of basic tools, they found the natural fracture lines of a rock which they cracked and filled with wood and water. When the wood expanded, the cracks deepened and they could continue to break huge blocks of stone which they shaped with absolute precision.

Their empire was so vast that relics of the Inca probably still lie hidden in the forest, untouched and undiscovered.

CONQUEST AND GOLD

In the early 1500s, European sailors arrived by ship to South America. These Spanish and Portuguese colonizers were called "**conquistadors.**" They were incredibly brutal, waging war on local communities. A Spaniard named Francisco Pizarro brought down the Inca Empire and took control of the land.

WATER ROADS

Descending into the complicated world of the Amazon rainforest can be deadly if you don't know how to manage it. There are no paths, so you have to slice through dense clusters of thick forest vines called lianas. The rivers are the easiest way through and this was how the conquistadors got around.

EL DORADO

Pizarro had heard the tale of a hidden city dripping in gold, hidden deep in the jungles of Peru. There were rumors that its people threw this precious metal into their lakes and their king even covered himself in gold dust every morning. They called it El Dorado. The stories of gold and fortune drove the newly-arrived invaders wild with excitement. Pizarro and his men set out in search, but it was a dangerous trip that left them empty-handed.

RUBBER BOOM

Invaders were also attracted by the rubber tree. Cutting small nicks in the bark makes a soft, milky liquid seep from the wound. This substance, called latex, can be burned with sulphur to make bouncy, strong rubber. By the 1830s, this had attracted many companies who rubbed their hands in glee at the thought of what they could do with it! Sadly, this rubber boom cost many lives and destroyed large areas of the forest.

HOW THE AMAZON GOT ITS NAME

The Amazon River was named by a Spanish conquistador, a soldier called Orellana. After battles with local communities, Orellana wrote home describing mighty warrior women. They reminded Orellana of the Amazons, the fearless female fighters in the ancient Greek myths. Today, we believe he may have encountered groups of Tapuya people.

INSPIRING AMAZON

The Amazon has inspired generations of scientists and artists. Despite many years of study, there is still much in the Amazon that is unknown to science. It is home to half of the world's tropical forests and 10% of the planet's biodiversity. Yet the thickness of the forest, added to the chances of simply getting lost (the canopy of trees stretches over a larger area than western Europe!) means that we can only guess at the number of species not yet examined. Why is it important to study the natural world? It can tell us about evolution, provide new medicines, and give us a better idea of the planet's future.

RAINFOREST FIELD TRIPS

To go on an expedition to the forest, you must be well-prepared. You'll need sunscreen, plenty of water, and a wide-brimmed hat to keep the creepy-crawlies off. Even though it is hot, it's useful to wear long pants to cover bare skin. Wear good shoes and high socks (for the ankle nibblers), a light, waterproof jacket, and take plenty of mosquito spray. Plus of course, any equipment you'll need to do your work. Remember to leave nothing behind!

BOTANICAL ARTIST

Margaret Mee (1909–1998) was a British **botanical** illustrator who made over 15 expeditions to the Amazon River. Mee could draw and paint plants in extraordinary detail. Through her work, she discovered the destruction being done to the forest during the building of the Trans-Amazonian highway. She was determined it would not go unnoticed. Mee used her art to raise international awareness about the Amazon and how important it is to conserve it. Today, photographers, filmmakers, writers, and sound artists show the beauty of the Amazon's wildlife and the danger it is facing.

EXPEDITIONS AND OBSERVATIONS

The Amazon Tall Tower Observatory (ATTO) is built high above the forest canopy. This is a research site for scientists from Brazil and Germany. Here they are gathering evidence and trying to answer questions like: how is the forest and the water cycle connected? How are they affected by greenhouse gases and climate change? Another way to gather information is by trekking into the jungle on scientific expeditions. Many expeditions uncover whole new species, like the lizard walking toad, a warty little thing which doesn't hop like a frog but scuttles. Or there's the three-inch fish (A. kullanderi), which is as colorful as a rainbow and lives in isolated waterfalls.

INDIGENOUS PEOPLE

There are over 400 **indigenous** societies in the Amazon, each with their own language, culture, and traditions. In the Amazon, these communities have traditional lives away from cities. Most learn to fish and hunt as children. They understand the true potential of the plants around them for food, tools, and medicine.

LARGEST AND SMALLEST

The Yanomami are the largest indigenous group of people living in relative isolation (population 35,000). The smallest is made up of just one man. He has resisted contact from the outside world for his entire life. Many societies in the Amazon region are uncontacted, meaning they have had no communication with people outside of the forest. Many don't want to.

PROTECTED LAND

Indigenous communities in the Amazon need the forest to survive. This is their home and their way of living. Areas called national parks have been created to protect parts of the forest for them. But there aren't enough and they often come under attack from loggers. The loggers illegally chop down wood or burn the land, which strips it of plants and wildlife.

RITUALS

Each group has their own celebrations, rituals, and ways of dressing. The Kayapo people have a special ritual for children called Bemp, when they are given their ancestral name. Older men and women will wear feathered headdresses that fan outwards. These represent the universe. The Kayapo are also known for their unique body paints. The women often wear yellow and black paint and ear and lip plugs. The ear plug is a sign that you are listening to someone, and the bigger the ear plug the more respect you are giving.

AWA

The Awa tribe were once completely nomadic. They moved around the forest, finding homes in different areas. Nowadays, only a handful continue to live in the forest. They are highly skilled at making everything they need from the forest itself, including baskets, nets, ornaments, and hunting equipment. The Awa are precise hunters, using handmade bows and arrows. But with their food comes a respect for what they eat. If the mother of an animal is shot down, they will often nurture and raise the young.

NAIA,
star of the water

Have you heard the story of the queen of lilies and how it came to be? Some say the first lily grew from a girl who lived in a village of the forest. Her name was Naia and she fell in love with the moon. Each night, she watched as it waxed and waned in the velvet black sky among the stars. Naia followed its light wherever she could. She climbed trees so that she might stand closer to its light. She walked to the tip of a mountain to try to touch its surface with outstretched hands.

One evening as she walked beside the river, Naia spied the moon glimmering. It swayed gently in the ripples as though waving for her to follow. Naia followed the welcoming light, but each time she reached out, the moon scattered and disappeared. She tried again and again until finally she didn't resurface.

The caring moon felt deeply sorry for Naia and so decided to give her the gift of a new life. Her arms began to stretch and widen into leaves, her back sprouted spines to keep her secure and her hair twisted down to feed off the riverbed. At dusk each night, her petals open to welcome in the moon's light.

LIFE ON THE RIVER

BOATS

Up and down the waterways of the Amazon, river boats chug, speed, or drift along peacefully. Over 34 million people live in the Amazon basin, from large cities like Belém on the coast to small towns and villages along its tributaries. Many people use the river to get from one place to another. It is also an important way of getting food and goods to sell and buy.

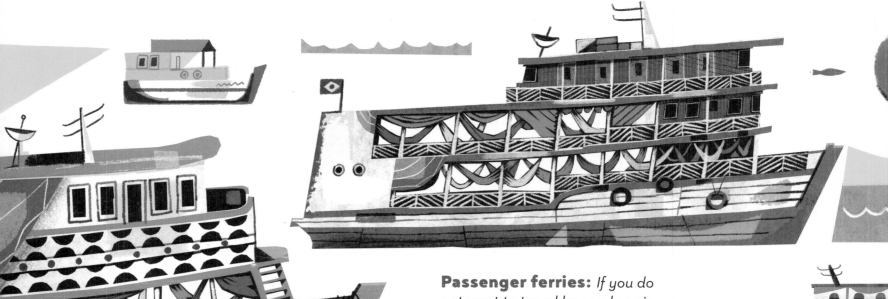

Passenger ferries: *If you do not want to travel by road or air, you can take a passenger ferry from the river mouth all the way up to Peru.*

Rafts: *Traditional wooden canoes and rafts made of light balsa wood. In Peru there is the Great River Amazon Raft Race where teams of four make their way down 120 miles of river.*

Speed boats: *Used to travel quickly along the river. They are sometimes tied up to larger boats and pulled along until they are needed.*

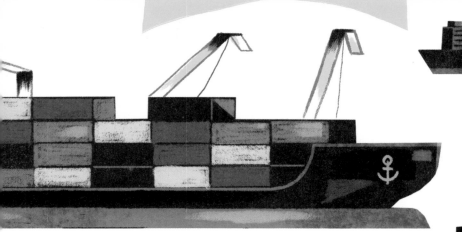

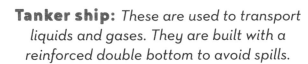

Tanker ship: *These are used to transport liquids and gases. They are built with a reinforced double bottom to avoid spills.*

Dry container ship: *Equipped with cranes so that the goods can be loaded and unloaded in any dock.*

Small cargo ships: *Cargo ships transport goods like bananas, pigs, and furniture. These are stored at the bottom, while on the upper decks passengers can lounge in hammocks.*

Medical boats: *Hospital ships go up and down the waterway with doctors and medical supplies. This is incredibly valuable for people living in remote villages far from a town or city.*

Barges and push boats: *Large steel containers are filled with food like grains. Lines of them are pushed up and down the waterways by push boats.*

Uba: *A particular type of canoe made from the wood of an entire tree trunk*

FISHING

The Amazon River is incredibly important in providing food for people. Fish is caught to eat at home or to sell. Areas where lots of fishing takes place are called fisheries. As in the seas, overfishing is a huge problem in the Amazon River. There are many schemes to control how people catch fish and the number that are caught.

Kayapo fisherman

BOW AND ARROW

An ancient fishing technique still practiced in the Amazon uses a bow and arrow. The bow is made of a light wood which can easily bend into a semicircle. This type of fishing is done in the daytime and requires extreme skill and precision.

NET FISHING

There are different types of net fishing to catch different types of fish.

Buoyed net A net is buoyed up in a stream of water and left there to catch all that crosses its path.

Cast net A net is thrown into the water to trap fish. Weights are woven into its rim so it falls and sinks into the water.

HARPOON FISHING

A harpoon is a wooden lance with a pointed tip attached by a cord. The tip releases with the cord and stays stuck in the fish. This is often used to catch large fish like the pirarucu.

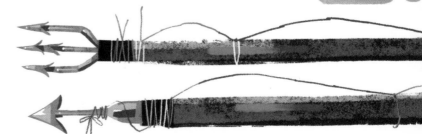

AMAZONIAN CITY

The city of Manaus is the capital of the Brazilian state of Amazonas. It was built in the heart of the jungle, on the banks of the river in a place where two huge tributaries come together. This area is called the meeting of the rivers and it is an incredible sight. Here we find the blackwater from the River Negro flowing out from the Colombian jungles to meet the whitewater of the River Solimões from the Andes.

Manaus was first built up as a small fort town in the height of the 1830s rubber boom. Today, it is a huge port city with ships sailing in from the Atlantic. The city is home to a beautiful opera house, botanical gardens, and important research centers like the National Research Institute of Amazonia.

Most of the large cities in the Amazon region, like Manaus and Iquitos, are positioned between blackwater rivers (which have fewer insects) and whitewater rivers (which are better for fishing). Smaller towns also dot the banks of the river, all with a close relationship to the water. In Peru there is a town called Santa Maria de Ojeal where the houses float! In the rainy season, the houses seem to sit above water and in the dry season, they are on stilts.

WATER POWER

Never underestimate the power of water. It can freeze solid, turn into a fine mist... and even make electricity. Up and down the Amazon River, huge dams have been built that collect river water and turn it into energy. Energy that is made from **renewable** sources is called green energy.

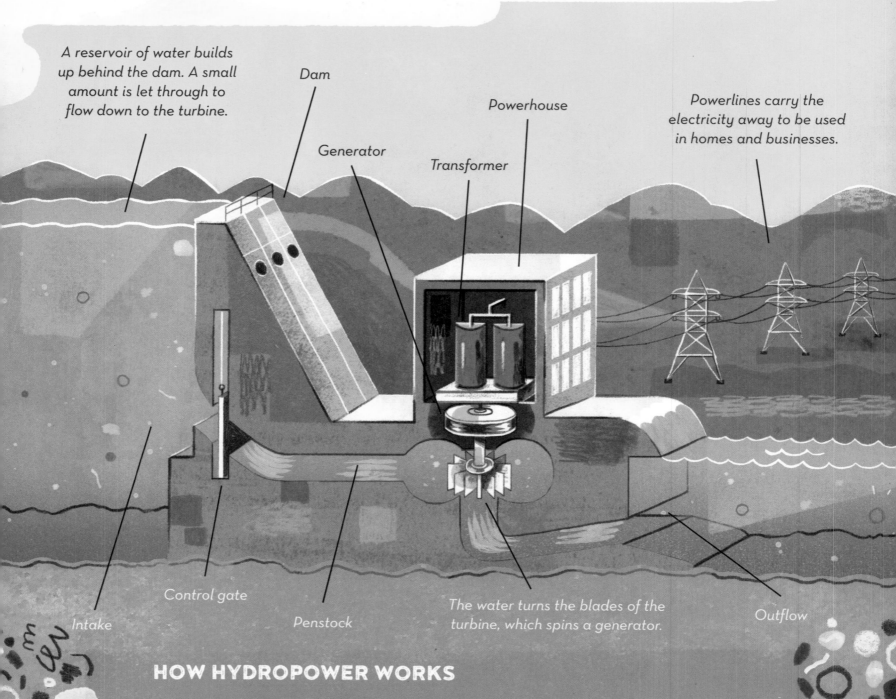

A reservoir of water builds up behind the dam. A small amount is let through to flow down to the turbine.

Dam

Generator

Powerhouse

Transformer

Powerlines carry the electricity away to be used in homes and businesses.

Control gate

Intake

Penstock

The water turns the blades of the turbine, which spins a generator.

Outflow

HOW HYDROPOWER WORKS

Making electricity from water is called **hydropower**. Water must be flowing fast to make energy, so dams are built to store it up. The water is channelled to turn huge turbines. A generator then converts the power into electricity.

HOW GREEN IS GREEN?

Building dams often floods areas which should not be flooded. This causes enormous disruption to the natural balance of the river system. It leads to a loss of animal and plant habitats and people's homes. It can stop the journey of fish up and down the river. This in turn affects the animals that need fish for food. The natural damage from hydro dams has come under criticism from indigenous communities and environmental groups who want them to stop being built.

DANGEROUS DAM

The Balbina dam in Brazil was built to make energy for local communities. But to do this, they flooded the forest. People were moved far away from their homes, animals weren't rescued from the water, and the trees were left to rot. The rotting plant matter is now releasing the greenhouse gases methane and carbon dioxide, which damage the environment. Is the amount of electricity made worth the damage?

THE AMAZON IN DANGER

From above, it is clear to see how a river connects things. It is a visible, watery road which stretches across borders. But the connection is much deeper than that, too. Connectivity is the idea that every tiny thing links up and is affected by the other. Across this book you will have seen trees, mammals, insects, and people that all connect to the river in a different way. Even those who do not live in or near the Amazon are being affected by it through the world's climate.

LOGGING

Logging, or cutting down trees to sell for their wood, is a major cause of **deforestation** in the Amazon basin. Chainsaws and bulldozers have been cutting back enormous blocks of forest that are sometimes bigger than whole countries. This deforestation is like peeling back the skin of the living planet.

A LONELY FOREST

Pulling down trees in large numbers can lead to patches of the forests becoming isolated from the rest. A lonely forest is not a happy one. Isolating patches like this leads to "fragmentation." Fragmentation means that the forest is broken up into pieces, which makes the movement of animals and plants very difficult.

MINING AND OIL

As well as trees, the forest contains other natural resources like gas and oil that we use as fuel. Huge mines have been dug to extract metal, leaving empty, muddy holes deep in the basin. Oil pipes have also been built carrying fuel for miles. If these break or leak, they can wreak terrible damage on the water and wildlife.

BURNING FOREST

Huge chunks of forest are being burned to clear the ground for cows to graze. In 2019, huge fires in the forest caused black, sooty rain to fall in the city of Sao Paulo, thousands of miles away. The rainforest is being reduced by the size of two football fields every single minute. This land is used for farming soy and beef.

CLIMATE ACTIVISTS

The Amazon is still very much in danger. But efforts to stop the river being polluted or turned into electric dams are being courageously fought. Protests and action to stop the forest being cut down are being led by indigenous communities, charities, aid groups, environmental organizations, and even individuals like you. There is still much to do to protect this precious space. It's important to remember that we can help. Each and every one of us can be a climate activist.

FIGHTING FOR OUR RIGHTS

In Brazil, indigenous leaders are marching for the planet and their homes. Free Land Camp is the largest gathering of indigenous leaders from all five of Brazil's regions. The protests demand protection of indigenous rights, and the protection of the forest and river. Deforestation on indigenous reserves is much lower than in the National Parks. Standing up for indigenous rights is standing up for the rights of the forest.

GLOBAL PROTEST

In 2018, the Swedish climate activist Greta Thunberg began a one-person school strike (skolstrejk) that soon became a worldwide movement. The Fridays For Futures protests have led to millions of people marching together to demand better climate protection, including for the Amazon, an essential part of our environment. Climate activists can do many things to make a positive change. Whatever you choose to do, large or small, you can show solidarity and make a difference too.

In 2020, over 130 million children and adults went on strike in over 7,500 cities. They demanded 100% renewable energy by 2030. The Fridays for Futures movement supports MAPA, the most affected people and areas, which includes people whose lives depend on the Amazon River and forest.

A RIVER OF THE WORLD

The story of the Amazon River is not just the story of one body of water, it's the story of everything that lives in it and around it, and uses it to survive. It is the home of over 3,000 species of fish. There are 1,300 species of birds. The forest itself is home to over 2.5 million species of insects and over 16,000 species of trees. Each living thing relies on the natural system it belongs to: the type of water, the soil, the rock, the insects, the fish, and the larger prey. Life here has evolved over millions of years to be utterly unique, and it is all connected. It is as though each living thing is attached by a tiny thread. A movement here or a jolt there shakes and disturbs all that is attached. You're connected, too.

Ask yourself: is the natural world a wondrous thing to you? Is it worth protecting? Is extinction acceptable? Is there a better way for us all to live together? They may seem like big questions and you may think you are too small. But if a drop of water can glide along a great river, then think of all the things that you could do.

GLOSSARY

Aquatic Growing or living in or near water.

Archaeologists People who study things that people in the past made and left behind.

Basin Area of land that is drained, or fed, by a large river and all the tributaries that run into it.

Biodiversity Variety of different plant and animal species.

Botanical Relating to the study of plants.

Camouflage Process of an animal's color or shape changing to match the surrounding environment.

Carbon dioxide Gas released when fossil fuels (like coal, oil, and gasoline) are burned.

Cartilage Firm, flexible tissue which makes up the skeletons of some fish, like sharks.

Colonialism When one country invades and takes control of another, ruling its people and taking its wealth for the benefit of the controlling country.

Condensation When water that is in the form of water vapour (a gas) becomes liquid water.

Conquistador A conqueror, especially the Spanish conquerors of Mexico and Peru in the 1500s.

Deforestation Cutting down trees in large areas, the destruction of forests by humans.

Downstream Direction of where the river is flowing to, with the current.

Ecosystem Community of all the living things in a place, and the environment around them.

Endemic Plant or animal that is only found in a certain area.

Estuary Place where a river joins the sea.

Evaporation Process where a liquid changes into a gas, particularly by heating it.

Extinction When an entire species, or type, of animal dies out.

Fauna Animals that live in a region, period, or special environment.

Flora Plants of a particular area, type of environment, or period of time.

Hydropower Making electricity through the force of fast-moving water.

Indigenous people Earliest inhabitants of a place and their descendants, usually with a unique cultural history which has been handed down the generations.

Precipitation Water that falls from the sky to the ground, as rain or snow.

Renewable Energy that doesn't use up the world's resources, but can be used time and time again, like power that comes from water, wind, or the Sun.

Source All rivers start at a source, a place where the water comes from. This could be melting snow, glaciers, or underwater springs.

Tidal bore Body of water that rushes up rivers or estuaries near the coast, especially at high tides.

Transpiration Process of losing water through a surface or the skin. On a plant this is through the leaves.

Tributary Freshwater stream or river that joins a main river rather than heading directly into the sea.

Upstream Direction of where the river begins, against the flow of water.

Water cycle Process that all water follows as it moves around Earth in different forms, such as liquid water, solid ice, or water vapor.

Water vapor Water that has turned into a gas.

WRITTEN BY SANGMA FRANCIS

In the summer of 2019, I had the immense fortune of visiting the Amazon river to research this book. It is an experience I will never forget. The forest is gargantuan, thick with noise and brimming with life. I saw spiders as big as my hand, pink dolphins swimming close by, funghi glowing in the dark, snakes, iguanas, monkeys and each morning I was greeted by a wild chorus of birds. Our boat drifted up the Cuierias tributary where trees sat beneath the flood waters, and while we chugged along I talked to ecologists, artists and botanists. I listened to professors who revealed how delicate yet truly extraordinary the Amazon is. Although we learn facts and numbers when we seek to know our world, the most important thing I have come to know is that it is a home. A home for insects, birds, wild cats, snakes, butterflies, and millions of people too. I hope I have done this home justice.

My gratitude goes to the organizers at LABVERDE, the National Institute of Amazonian Research (INPA) and the Adolpho Ducke Reserve. A special thank you also to everyone involved in the making of this; the publisher for supporting my research, the editors, designers and team of people behind every book. Thank you also to Rômolo whose artwork is a treasure worthy of the mighty Amazon.

Sangma Francis is a writer of fiction and nonfiction books for children. She has written five books for Flying Eye, including *Everest* and the *Secret Lives of...* series. When she isn't writing, she can be found swimming in lakes, rivers, and the sea.

ILLUSTRATED BY RÔMOLO D'HIPÓLITO

When I started working on this book, I was also on a pleasant mission of transforming a square's empty lot into a community garden with native plants and flowers. It was wintertime here in Brazil, and I could see the blossoming of both these projects across the next seasons. From my studio, I saw sprouting from my drawings colorful birds and fishes, spotted wild cats and snakes, all sorts of greens, and, of course, large amounts of water. Outside, on that sleeping ground, I saw the first flights of native bees and hummingbirds over the first yellowish pumpkin flowers, also tomatoes and beans spreading their roots all across the lot, and two passion fruits climbing two pieces of old broomsticks. These two experiences guided me to think about the act of sowing and reaping and how I can contribute to the rainforest I want for the future. Beyond political and geographical boundaries, I think of the Amazon as an idea that we all can carry and spread like seeds.

It was a great pleasure to be on board with this talented team. A special thanks to Lilly Gottwald and Satu Hämeenaho-Fox, who accompanied me on each page of this book, and Sangma Francis, who shares with me this delightful expedition along the Amazon River.

Rômolo is an award-winning Brazilian artist and illustrator. In 2019, he received the Special Mention award at the Golden Pinwheel Young Illustrators Competition (Shanghai), and in 2018, he was selected for the Ibero-America official catalogue (Mexico). On Sundays, you can find him at the community garden between friends and rufous-bellied thrushes.

Other Books in the Series

EVEREST
By Sangma Francis and Lisk Feng

There is a place where a mountain grows. It is the highest spot on Earth, the ultimate challenge for mountain-climbing adventurers, the towering figure of Sagarmatha, the Goddess of the Sky...

Welcome to Mount Everest.

In this stunning book, travel back to the mountain's ancient origins, learn about the flora and fauna of its great flanks, and discover the rich culture and history surrounding it.

THE GREAT BARRIER REEF
By Dr Helen Scales and Lisk Feng

In the waters where Australia meets the vast Pacific Ocean, grows the world's most famous reef. Schools of fish dart among the colorful corals, octopuses hide in dark corners, and sharks patrol the clear waters above.

Welcome to the Great Barrier Reef.

In this glowing illustrated guide, discover the plants, animals, and people that live and work in this vast underwater treasure trove.

This first US edition published in 2021 by Flying Eye Books,
an imprint of Nobrow Ltd. 27 Westgate Street, London E8 3RL.

Illustrations © Rômolo D'Hipólito 2021.
Text © Sangma Francis 2021.

Rômolo D'Hipólito and Sangma Francis have asserted their
right under the Copyright, Designs and Patents Act, 1988,
to be identified as the Illustrator and Author of this Work.

Published in the US by Nobrow (US) Inc.

Printed in Poland on FSC® certified paper.

ISBN: 978-1-912497-75-1

Order from www.flyingeyebooks.com